Back to Basics

SCIENCE

for 5–6 year olds

Godfrey Hall

Letts

Who am I?

Fill in the spaces or put a tick ✔ in the correct box.

My name is ____________________________.

I am a boy ☐ girl ☐

My eyes are		My hair is	
brown	☐	black	☐
blue	☐	brown	☐
green	☐	blonde	☐
grey	☐	red	☐

I am ____________ centimetres tall.

I weigh ____________ kilogrammes.

My shoes are size ____________.

There are ____________ people in my home.

What do I need?

To stay alive we need food and water. Help the pirate find his way to the food and water.

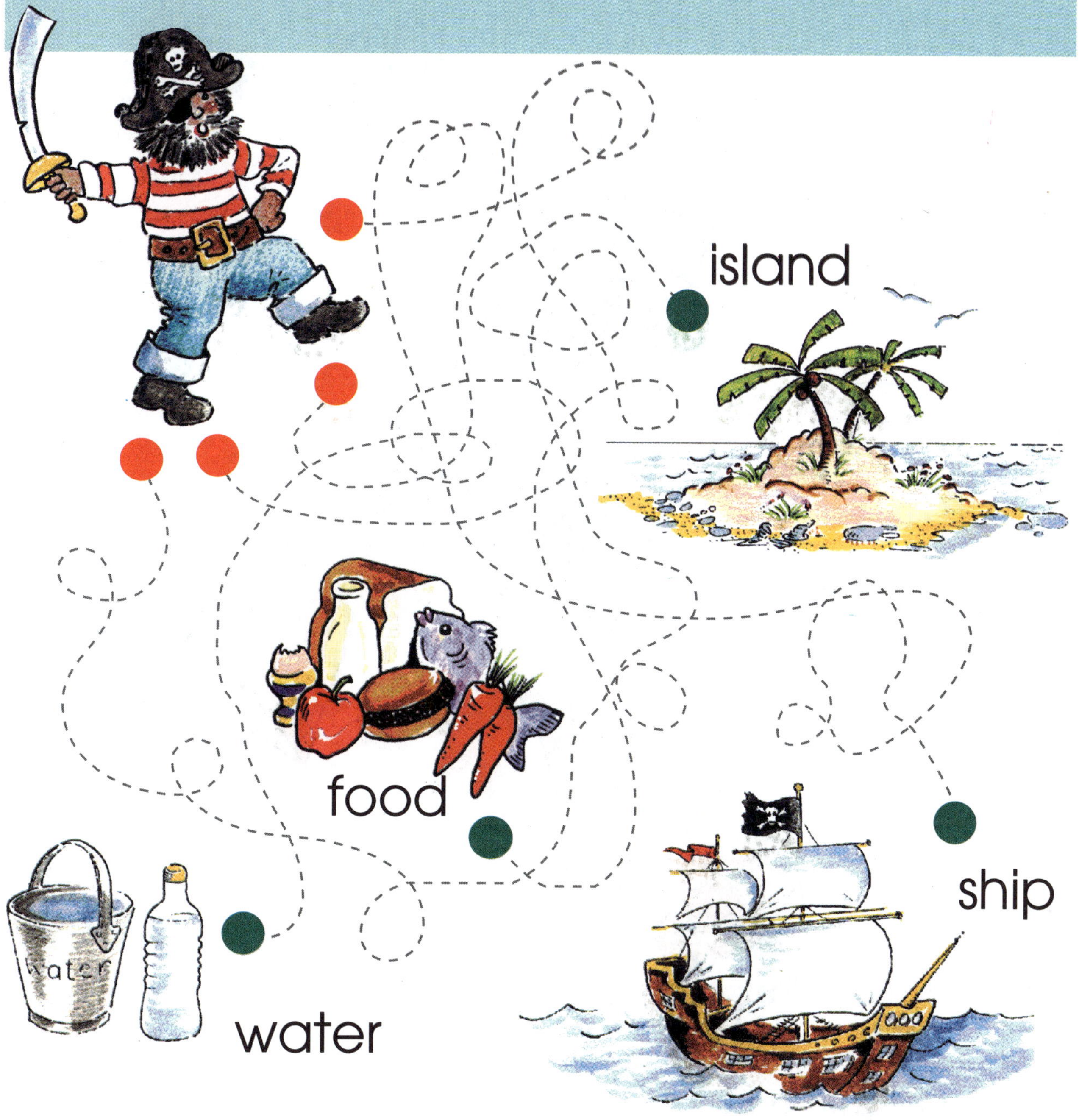

The body

Name the parts of the body. Fill in the spaces using the words below.

head foot arm hand leg finger

Draw a picture of yourself.

A plant

Name the parts of a plant. Fill in the spaces using the words below.

root petal leaf flower stem

Colour in the plant.

Find out the names of some flowers near your home.

Where do they live?

Where do these animals live? Write **land**, **sea** or **air** in the spaces. Put the animals into sets.

sea

___ ___ ___ ___

___ ___ ___

___ ___ ___ ___

___ ___ ___

___ ___ ___

___ ___ ___ ___

___ ___ ___

Homes

Match the creature with its home.

bird

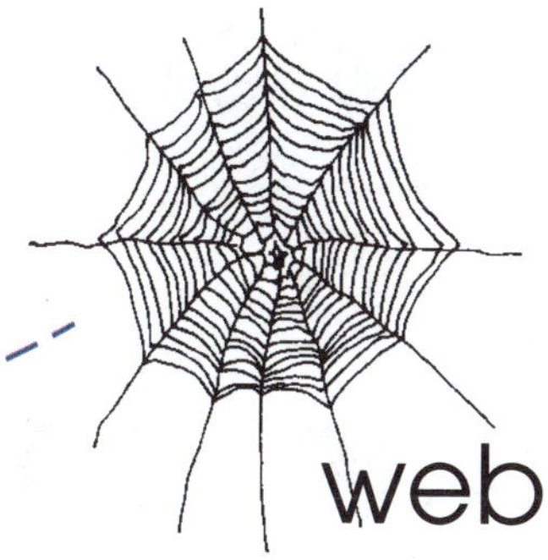

web

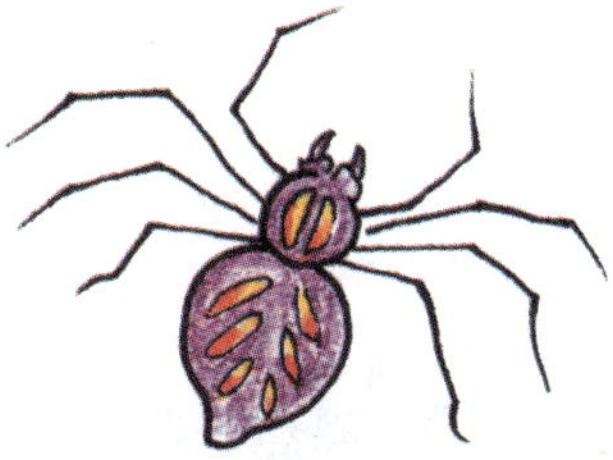

spider

water

basket

fish

worm

nest

dog

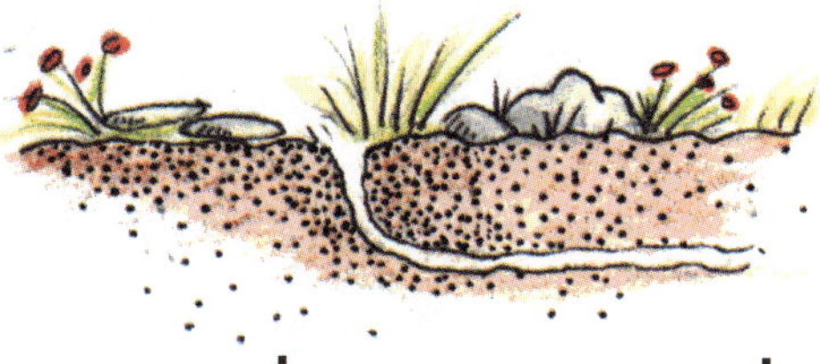

underground

Living and non-living

Sort out the living and non-living things. Draw them in the boxes below.

living

non-living

What makes a plant grow?

Draw a ring round three of the things a plant needs to help it grow.

sand

oil

salt

light

heat

water

Grow your own cress. Put some cress seeds on damp cotton wool. Put this on a saucer. Put the saucer in a sunny place. Keep the cotton wool damp. Watch what happens after a few days.

Hard or soft

Which things are hard and which are soft? Put a tick ✔ in the correct box.

hard ☐
soft ☑

hard ☑
soft ☐

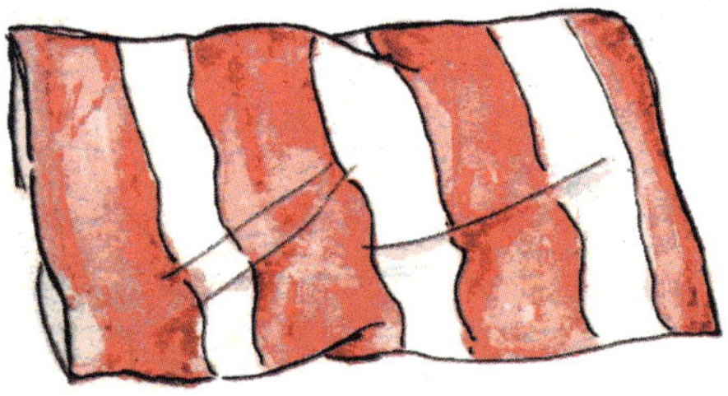

☐ hard
☐ soft

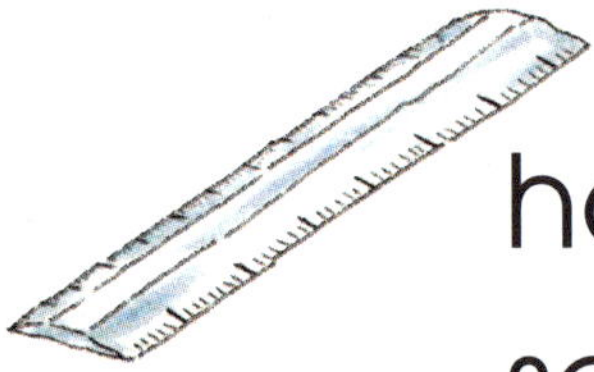

hard ☐
soft ☐

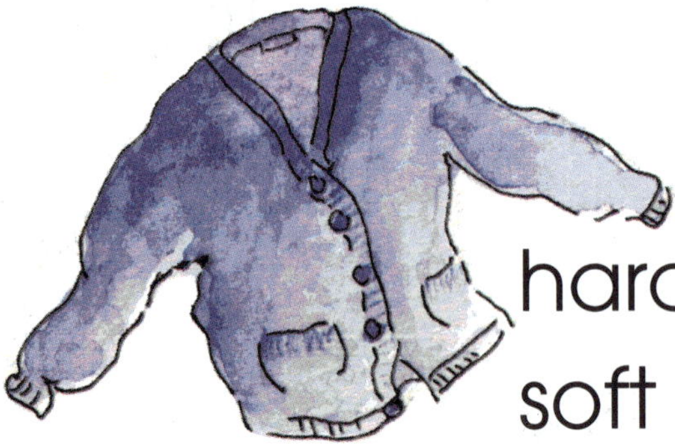

hard ☐
soft ☐

hard ☐
soft ☐

☐ hard
☐ soft

☐ hard
☐ soft

Hot or cold

Colour the hot things red.

Colour the cold things blue.

Weather chart

Fill in this weather chart for a week.

day	is it sunny, cloudy or raining?	is it hot or cold?
Monday		
Tuesday		
Wednesday		
Thursday		
Friday		
Saturday		
Sunday		

Keep another weather chart for two weeks.

Weather clothes

When do you wear these clothes?
Put a tick ✔ in the correct box.

☐ rain
☐ sun
☐ snow

☐ rain
☐ sun
☐ snow

☐ rain
☐ sun
☐ snow

Colour in the pictures.

Rubbish

Find the right homes for your rubbish.

Where do you put your rubbish?

Paper, wood or glass

Which are paper? Put a **p** in the box.
Which are wood? Put a **w** in the box.
Which are glass? Put a **g** in the box.

Where does light come from?

Draw a red ring round the things that give us light.

Colour in the picture.

Sounds

Match the animal with the sound it makes.

What sounds can you hear in your home?

Good or bad

Which of these sounds are good?
Which of these sounds are bad?
Put a tick ✔ by the good sounds
and a cross ✘ by the bad sounds.

A bird singing. ☑

Lots of cars, vans and lorries. ☐

Someone playing the piano. ☐

Someone laughing. ☐

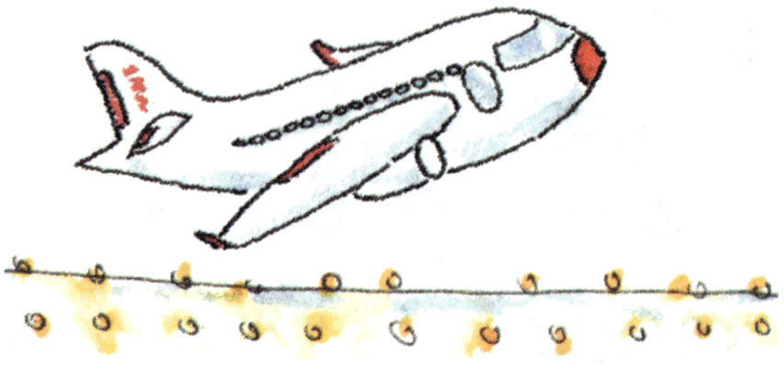

A plane taking off. ☐

Electricity

Ring the things found in your **home** worked by electricty.

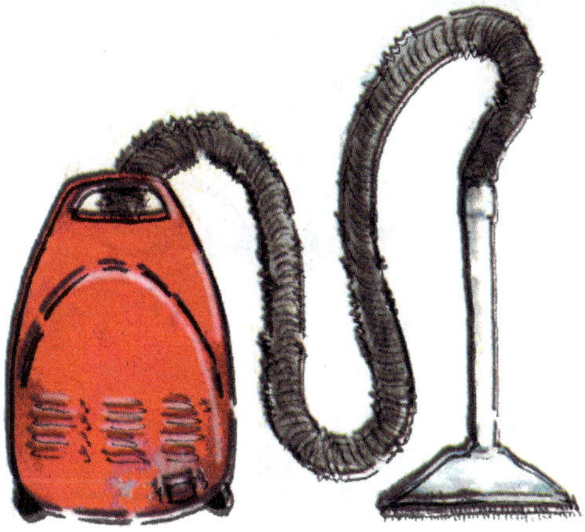

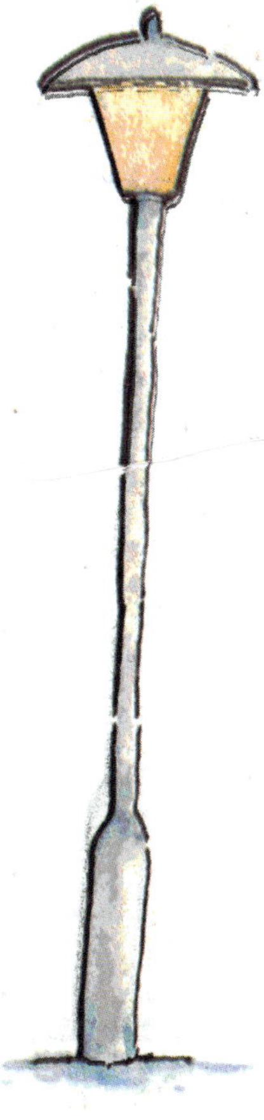

All these things work by electricity.

Magnets

Put a tick ✔ by the things that stick to a magnet.

If you have a magnet, test them.

Traffic lights

Write down which colours are showing... red, orange or green.

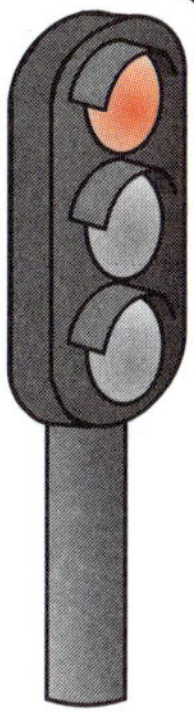

red

The face

Name the parts of the face. Fill in the spaces with the words below.

hair eye nose mouth neck ear

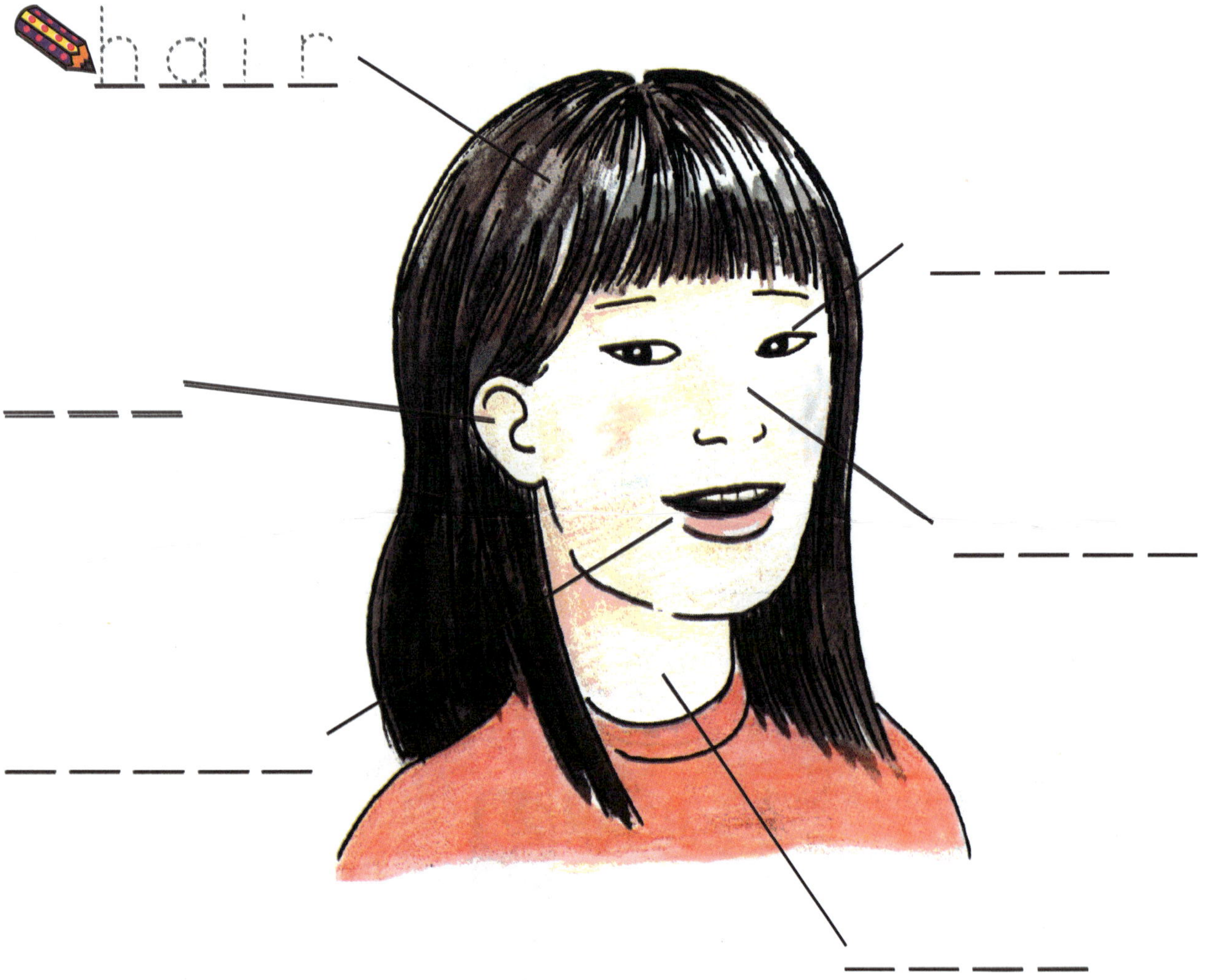

Which sense?

We have five senses.
We can hear. We can see.
We can smell. We can taste.
We can feel.
Draw something you can...

hear

see

smell

taste

feel

Pushing and pulling

Write **push** by the things you push.
Write **pull** by the things you pull.

push

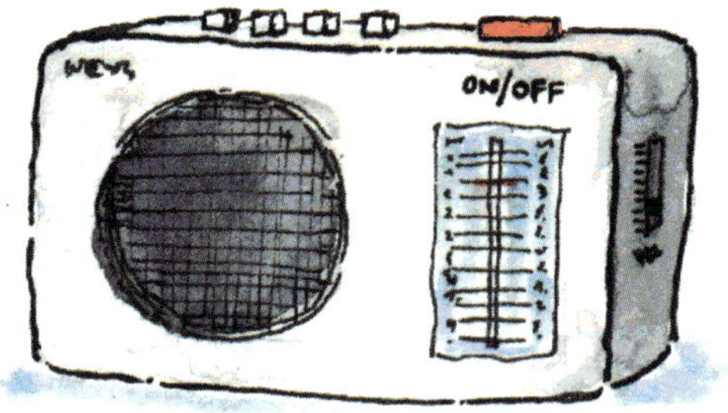

What other things can you push or pull in your home?

Heavy and light

Draw a ring round the heavy things.

Mixing colours

What happens when you mix colours together? Colour these in.

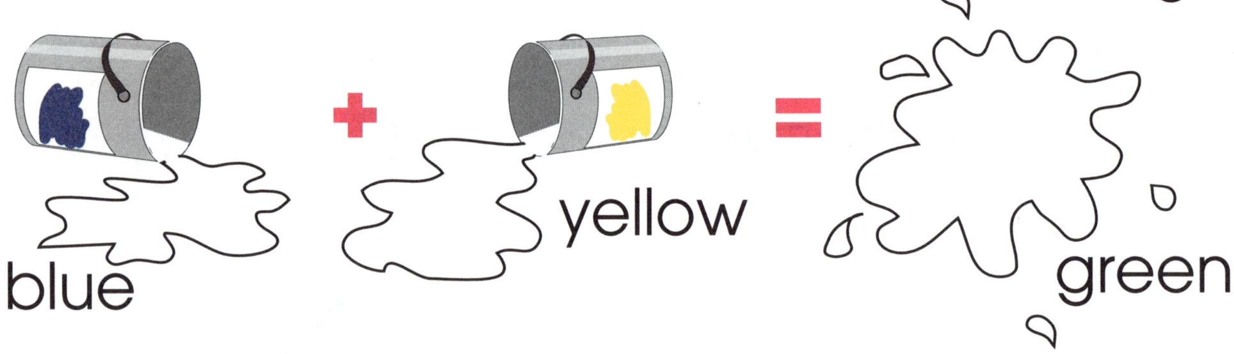

Try mixing two colours of your own.

Vegetables and fruit

Write a **v** on the vegetables and an **f** on the fruits. Colour them in.

Grow a carrot top. Put a carrot top in a saucer of water. Put it somewhere light and warm. Keep it wet. What happens after a week?

Good or bad

Put a tick ✔ by the foods you think are good for you.

apple ✔

burger ☐

chips ☐

cream cake ☐

salad ☐

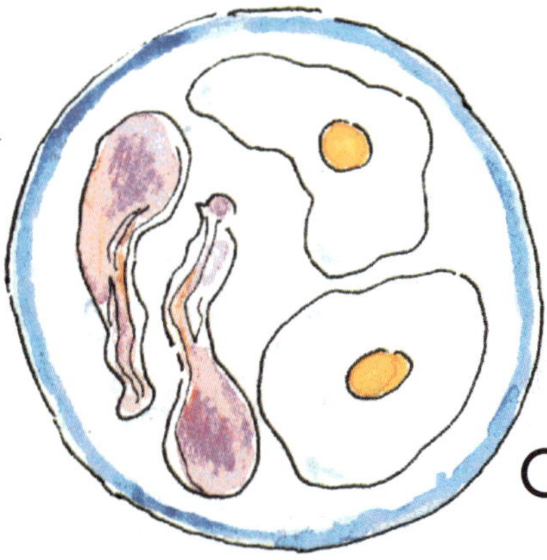

carrot ☐

fried eggs and bacon ☐

What is your favourite food?

Looking after our world

It is important that we look after our world. Draw a ring round the children who are **not** doing this.

How can you help to look after where you live?

Pond life

Put a tick ✔ by the creatures that live in a pond.

fish ☐

duck ✔

☐ spider

horse ☐

newt ☐

ladybird ☐

frog ☐

snail ☐

What is it made of?

Help Little Red Riding Hood find a path to the four tiny houses made of brick, mud, glass and stone. Fill in the spaces.

What other things can you use to build a home?

Day and night

Look at these two pictures. Draw a ring round anything that has changed in the second picture.

day

night